THE INTENTIONAL CONSULTANT

Devona E. G. Williams, Ph.D.

ISBN: 1468002228
ISBN-13: 978-1468002225

DEDICATION

The Intentional Consultant, is dedicated to my brother, Russell Goeins, who wanted me to write a book called *The Consultant's Consultant*. He felt that, from what he observed, I had developed a business consulting practice that made it look relatively easy and that I had a process, strategy, and ideas from which other consultants or business people could benefit. That was some ten years ago.

My brother is no longer with me but his idea has stuck with me. Now after 22 years in business, I feel the need to share more broadly my own experiences and processes that will benefit people who intend to become business consultants or further develop their consulting practice.

TABLE OF CONTENTS

ACKNOWLEDGMENTS

I'd like to acknowledge the special people in my life who continue to inspire me to grow my dream into a sustainable consulting practice. I give special thanks to my son who encouraged my small entrepreneurial endeavors in little ways very early on. Deserving of thanks also are my best friends and chief supporters, Deborah Gaines and Shirley Bryson. My mentors, Jim Anderson and Lozelle DeLuz, have played major roles in encouraging and inspiring my business pursuits. Special accolades go to my father, Russell Goeins, Sr., who encouraged my entrepreneurial spirit and gave me the courage to fight for my rightful place in the world, and to my mother, Viddie Goeins, who taught me to dream big. Finally, thanks to my sister, Lorrie Goeins, for her undying loyalty and my husband, Kenneth Anderson, who shares my dream.

1

WHY DO YOU WANT TO BE A CONSULTANT?

I am doing exactly what I want to do and what I prepared to do—I am living my dream! I always wanted to be a consultant, a management consultant, even with my very first professional job. On my journey, I prepared myself academically and made selective career choices that led me to develop a business blueprint for a sustainable consulting practice. It is no accident that I've been in this business for 22 years. Where I am today is the result of a thoughtful strategy and the desire to be an entrepreneur—specifically a business management consultant.

This book is intended for individuals who have a strong desire to provide their expertise in the form of business consulting and generate sufficient income for a livelihood. Independent consultants enjoy the idea of independence and understand that there is a strong entrepreneurial element that goes into sustaining a practice.

If you have purchased this book, most likely you are seeking new ideas, looking for something fresh and a way to "make it" with your own resources. This book comes from my own trials and errors, ideas, creativity and real life experiences; it comes from my heart. I share my secrets of success and strategies that I have used to grow my consulting business into a sustainable practice. It's my vision that this book will be used as a resource to inspire and motivate would-be consultants and entrepreneurs to think differently about what can done with their talents, skills, and resources.

Quite frankly, when you have a plan for your life and you stay positive, you can achieve sustained success despite the odds. When you're focused, you can accomplish great things—even those things that are hard. Your plan requires a vision, and the ability to plan, using resources around you, to make changes in your life and the lives of other people.

My best friend says that I am one of the few people she knows who actually puts together a plan, follows it through, and afterwards can look back and have something to show for that plan. And that's what I think is my gift—to develop focused personal, business, and life plans, put them in writing, commit to the plan, process, and execute!

I hope that the information I provide in this book will inspire and encourage you to begin and grow your consulting business into a sustainable enterprise. When you put your shoulder to the grindstone and follow your own strategies and vision for success you can become an intentional consultant.

Many people today say they are consultants. And in fact, the consulting industry gets a bad rap because it is often viewed as a holding place for people who are leaving private industry, perhaps because of downsizing, until they find a "real" job. It is also a place for professors and moonlighters who want to make extra income. It is often a special title reserved for people who sell cosmetics, or cars, or dabble in "get rich schemes." Sometimes these so-called consultants work on commission only or for little or no money.

There are many kinds of business consultants today who make relatively good incomes in niches ranging from finance, human resources, organizational, business services, to weddings. Political figures often end their careers by becoming consultants after holding elected or appointed office. One of the biggest challenges for consultants is the ability to engender trust. The American Management Association says that after used car salesmen and lawyers, consultants are the professionals least trusted by the consuming public.[1] Perhaps it is because the public views the profession as relatively unstable and unregulated.

To be a consultant, to be able to make a real income that can support yourself and your family, to make a bona fide living, is quite a different story.

---

[1] American Management Association, Public Relations training

To become a full time consultant, whatever the specific area of service, you must carefully define what it is you do and what you have to offer—and to whom. It is imperative that you think carefully about your consulting niche, focus, or specialty. People hire consultants to perform a service, in a personalized way, that they cannot perform on their own.

When I speak about being a consultant, I'm talking about making a living as a consultant with a minimum of a six-figure income that can pay your bills, take care of your family, send your children to college, help you drive a nice car, save for retirement, and maybe even have a business practice that you can sell someday. I'm also talking about creating a brand and business entity that evolves from an independent consultancy to a business practice that can leave a legacy for your children and community.

You probably bought this book because you want to become a consultant. Let me suggest a few things to think about.

- Why do you want to be a consultant?
- What is it that you will be consulting about?
- Who will your clients be?
- Why will they come to you?
- Why will they pay you?
- How can you quit your day job to be able to work as a consultant full-time?
- What do you need to do to be able to build the consulting practice to sustain it over time?

These are some of the core questions that this book will address. I will share the critical elements with you, based on my experience over the years. And I will share some tips along the way.

Many people dream about owning a business, but what some people don't realize is that all businesses start small. And unlike many other businesses that sell products, consultants sell themselves. If you believe that you can be a business consultant, that you have skills that can be turned into services of some sort that clients will be willing to buy, then you can become a business consultant. You can become an intentional consultant.

An intentional consultant is a person who plans a consulting practice and builds it for sustainability. That's my definition. It is not happenstance. It is not accidental. It is not something that you do until you find another job. It is what you choose to do to develop a sustainable livelihood for yourself. And it can happen, but you must follow a process and be committed to it, and probably work harder than most people, especially early on. But as we will see, the rewards are there.

To change your dream into reality you must follow the process. Some of the process steps include preparing yourself to be a consultant—things like gathering experiences, developing your initial business plan, and building your credentials. I will share the process that I have used, one that I think if you adopt will work for you as well.

Next we will take a look at the demand for your services—what you have to offer. In order for people to buy from you they are buying from you personally. Therefore, consultants must establish credibility and reliability with their clients and most of all establish a niche that is inextricably tied to their own skill set. That niche must also be something that is market-driven now and into the future so the consultant will be able to obtain reasonable fees and make a living. Marketing the consulting niche and maintaining a reputation are important elements of becoming a successful consultant and sustaining a business over time. Marketing your business is an essential element of developing and establishing your niche and your brand. This book will address marketing strategies that will be useful for the intentional consultant.

The marketing function is an ongoing aspect of business management that requires regular and consistent effort. Reputation must be managed and built in a positive direction over time. Your company and your practice will evolve as you do. Over time you introduce new services and products and move through transitions—all of which will need to be communicated to your past, current, and future clients.

It would really be great if being a consultant meant that all you have to do was hang a shingle out on your front door and tell people you are open for business. But it's not as simple as that. Consultants, like all other business owners, must manage their business. There are three elements of business: selling what you offer; managing your business or your operation; and developing your business. At all times as a business consultant you must manage and balance all three of these aspects. This is particularly challenging because the typical business consultant begins as a solo-entrepreneur. I will share my experiences in this area and give you some ideas for how to juggle these three elements.

Over the course of my time in business I have seen many independent business consultants go out of business. I call this *jumping ship*. Jumping ship is the term I use to describe the people who leave the independent world of business consulting and decide to take a "real" job because they cannot support themselves from the income they generate. I believe that if you have a good foundation for your consulting business you will not have to jump ship. A good foundation means:

- having a solid business plan;
- paying close attention to the marketplace and your clients;
- managing the three elements of business successfully; and
- building safeguards into your business that make your practice.

A firm foundation means that you are not just the *consultant of the day* but you have a long-term business practice that can become a sustainable company. The chapter on sustainability will talk about dealing with business transition challenges and how to sustain your practice for the long haul. I believe that the desire of most independent business people is to be able to have a business that can last a generation or more.

Consultants with sustainable businesses are always looking to the future, so this book ends with the chapter, *"What's Next?"* Here you will get a collection of ideas about how to generate new business and stay fresh. Who knows? Maybe your next business will not be a consulting business but a different type of business.

2

GROWING INDEPENDENCE THROUGH ENTERPRISE:

MY STORY

I think I've always wanted to be an entrepreneur. Even as a child, I always wanted to own a business. The idea of making money, being paid for my skills and talents as an independent person was instilled in me by my parents when I was young. I grew up having to do chores around the house, for which I earned an allowance. But for extra household chores, the hard things that the other children didn't want to do, my mother was willing to pay an extra five or ten cents. I was the one who always welcomed the chance to earn the extra income for performing these chores. The fact is that I had such a habit of doing this that my brother, who was thirteen years older, was able to borrow money from me!

My entrepreneurial experiences were varied. I collected soft drink bottles and returned them to the grocery store for the deposit—a nickel apiece. With my creative talents I used to write plays, make puppets, and put on puppet shows for the neighborhood kids. I charged the neighborhood children to come and watch my shows for five cents apiece. I lived on the third floor of our family home and found a way to charge my sisters a few cents to come upstairs. I created small rent slips on pieces of colored paper that I put into a small plastic vegetable basket. I tied a string to it, lowered it over the banister to the second floor. My sisters would select a rental slip and tug on the string to let me know that they were ready to come up to the third floor. Once they took their rental slip, they placed small change into the basket, usually a penny or two.

At the age of eight, I had a life-changing experience with my father. My dad, who nurtured my entrepreneurial spirit, always worked three jobs. He also had some sort of a business venture on the side and was an inventor of sorts. One such venture was a water ice truck he purchased to earn extra income. The water-ice truck featured ice (cherry, grape, and lemon) in paper cones, along with soft pretzels and mustard. The truck was painted on the outside with bright colors and images of what was sold and played a musical jingle to appeal exclusively to young children. He took me along with him on his route through the neighborhoods, and my job was to serve water ice and soft pretzels to the children who came up to the window of the truck. My favorite part was taking their sticky nickels and dimes and putting it in the change belt I wore around my waist. At the end of our shift my dad always gave me "a little cut" for the work that I had done. We would count the change together and he would give me the portion I earned. I think from that moment on I was smitten with the idea of owning and operating a business. I learned that if you work hard serving your clients you will be paid for what you do.

It didn't hurt that I had other entrepreneurs in my family. My uncle owned a number of party stores in Detroit, Michigan. During the summers when we visited him, I was the one who liked to work at the cash register and wait on clients. My uncle was a self-made man who grew wealthy from the businesses he created. He always seemed to have extra cash, and I made the connection early that having extra income was tied to owning a successful business. My brother was also an entrepreneur and, like my uncle, owned a number of businesses including a wig shop, an ice cream store, and a minimart. I worked at my brother's stores from time to time when I would visit him during the summers.

When I was in high school, I learned some valuable lessons about being an entrepreneur and having a business. We didn't always have what we wanted in our family of five children with our stay-at-home mom, but we always had what we needed. While in high school I was interested in getting involved in many activities such as school dances and class trips that were beyond our family budget. Although I received a weekly allowance to cover my school expenses and incidentals, my mother gave me a choice of how I wanted to use it.

I learned that by thinking creatively, I could stretch my dollars and increase my income through my entrepreneurial business activities. Instead of using my allowance to buy tokens to take the bus to school and lunch in the cafeteria, I rode my bike and packed my lunch. I used the money I saved from my allowance and babysitting to purchase packs of chewing gum from the grocery store and sell to other students by the piece. Because I was a talented seamstress, I sewed dresses for my mother's friends, for which I was paid. I used the fabric scraps to make patchwork quilt purses that I sold to my classmates.

I was able to leverage the five dollars a week of allowance into twenty dollars with the different entrepreneurial activities. In other words, I learned that by being a little bit more creative than other people and taking some risk, I was able to make more money than my peers at the age of 16.

My entrepreneurial desires didn't stop there. Art was a serious hobby for me as a child and I studied in art league during grade school and won quite a few contests and awards along the way. During my high school career, I elected to take art as an additional major along with my college prep studies. I sold my first painting thanks to a teacher-mentor who encouraged my painting and arranged a commissioned sale for fifty dollars. That was a lot of money for a high school student in 1972!

I went on to attend an out-of-state university, initially majoring in art and then changing my major to art education. I began college at the age of 17 and was a self-supporting student, responsible for all costs of my education. I received substantial academic scholarships my freshman year but as sophomore year approached, I turned to my entrepreneurial instincts to bolster my limited funding. Work-study jobs on campus were helpful but did not meet the full extent of my financial need. I learned that I could put some of my entrepreneurial ideas to work to help finance my college education. I worked many part-time jobs, using my variety of talents and experience to earn income. I parlayed my baton twirling skills, dance and cheerleading skills from high school into a majorette/cheerleading job with the city Parks and Recreation Department. I was able to convince the same department to hire me to teach arts and crafts classes on Saturday and after school drop-in programs for elementary students. I even used my piano playing skills to teach music classes. I quickly had a full schedule with Parks and Recreation and well-paying part-time employment that lasted more than ten years with progressive administrative responsibilities.

I learned to budget my income to buy additional art supplies beyond what was required for my classes. I created paintings, made jewelry and dolls. I used the art classes that I took to refine my skills. I sold commissioned and non-commissioned acrylic, watercolor, and oil paintings through word of mouth, art fairs, and street shows. I also came up with the idea to create African-American greeting cards for Christmas based on my own family (a unique concept at the time). With a small business plan, I was able to create a catalog of my cards, and obtained the envelopes and packaging wholesale. I used the catalog to persuade several shops on Main Street in my campus town, as well as the university bookstore, to carry my greeting cards on consignment. Some of these same stores also accepted my handmade dolls and jewelry on consignment. So with painting, greeting cards, and craft sales, I was able to supplement my college income as well as pay for a trip to Jamaica on spring break of my sophomore year! I continued developing my art talent, displaying and selling my art and crafts for many years in several other business ventures that will not be explored in detail in this book.

It should be noted here that I continued to work several part-time jobs throughout my college career—anywhere from 25 to 35 hours a week. I was a full-time student who graduated on time with a decent GPA!

In retrospect, I see that it's not enough to have skills or talent that can be converted in the form of a service or product that someone is willing to buy. One must be creative and a bit of a risk-taker to figure out how to convert the skills and talents into a business endeavor that will produce income. Creativity and innovation are a critical aspects of entrepreneurship and must be a part of a bigger plan with goals and objectives. Risk taking and visualizing the end result are needed abilities of any entrepreneur. These attributes are also needed by a consultant. So an intentional consultant must also be an entrepreneur.

The Seed of My Dream

At the age of 19, I got married and continued working and pursuing full-time academic studies at the university. I was able to graduate on time with more credits than were required for my art education major. I learned shortly before my graduation that I was pregnant with my first and only child. Because I was a working student I had no trouble finding full-time employment. My only problem was that, when I graduated back in 1976, few people wanted to hire a pregnant woman. While it was illegal to discriminate against women in employment, employers found ways to discourage pregnant women and women with infants and small children in the workforce. Child daycare was becoming more readily available but finding suitable, inexpensive care was also challenging. I encountered these problems as I sought employment. Once again it became essential for me to draw upon my entrepreneurial foundation and begin thinking about how I could someday own and operate my own business so that I would not be subject to the hiring whims of other people.

After graduating, I obtained my first job, which was a fairly good position, but when I reached my eight month of pregnancy I was asked to leave the job because my appearance offended some of the older people in the workplace (yes—firing or being "asked" to resign a job when pregnant was still a reality for many women in the 1970s, although it was illegal). While caring for my baby and collecting unemployment, I started to look into ways that I might become more entrepreneurial. Some of this effort included looking at my artwork as a potential source of income again. Although I had earned my college degree, it never occurred to me that I would encounter employment discrimination because I was married with a baby. I asked myself, *Could I get paid for selling my paintings? Could I write? What were some of the things I could do?* I knew that I had a burning desire to own and operate my own business one day.

By the time my son was a year old, I was 22. I was able to secure full-time employment, with benefits, in a good position with local government that allowed me to expand my skills by managing an organization and people. In this role as director of the Retired Senior Volunteer Program for New Castle County, I believe I was the youngest administrator in the nation. This program was funded in part by the federal agency, ACTION, with a local match from the county. We were part of a district office that included Baltimore, to which I traveled regularly to attend training. Some of the training included what was then a relatively new concept, managing-by-objectives, and soft skills training such as assertiveness. I was introduced then to managing-by-objectives, goal-setting, and the process of planning, and I have loved it ever since. I found that as my career grew that I became better and better at planning and implementation. I had the vision that perhaps one day I would be able to have a business that focused on planning and helping people increase their effectiveness in the planning process.

The seed of the idea for my business started when I was 24, but it was not until I took my next position that it came into focus. The position of RSVP director was eliminated from county government because of funding cuts. Because of the relationship I had established with the ACTION district office, my role was transferred to a state agency that administered VISTA, another ACTION funded program. In 1978, I found myself the statewide director for the VISTA program in the Office of Economic Opportunity in the Department of Community Affairs. In that role I was responsible for VISTA as well as several other anti-poverty programs. Many of these programs required a contractor to conduct program evaluations. In my role, I provided oversight for these evaluations.

I met with the first evaluator, and when he explained the process that would be used to assess the planned goals and objectives against actual progress, I was hooked. I knew I was adding another piece to the puzzle of the type of business I wanted to have. I was so excited to be exposed to program evaluation that I made the decision then and there to return to school to obtain my master's degree. I earned my master's degree in public administration with a specialization in agency management. Part of my study involved understanding program evaluation, organizational theory, planning, budgeting, and personnel management.

I continued to progress in administrative and executive roles in the early part of my career. The seed of my dream was to be a management/business consultant focusing on planning, organizational effectiveness, and program evaluation. I was determined to continue advancing my career in other areas because I felt that in order for me to be a credible consultant I needed to have more career experience in managing programs, organizations, and people. I started to see the seed of my dream germinate when I landed my first paid consulting assignment while working on my master's degree.

Following the completion of my master's degree, I was fortunate enough to receive a presidential management internship appointment in Washington as a political and policy analyst as well as budget analyst in various positions. One of those positions was in the Office of Management and Budget in which I was responsible for making recommendations on contracting activities for the federal government. This was pay dirt for me! I was able to see all of the proposals that were submitted by prospective consultants for various services for the federal government and learned the elements and appearance of well-prepared professional service proposals and the credentials needed by consultants to carry out the work.

When I worked in Washington, DC, I held positions in three different federal agencies over a two-year period and functioned very much like an in-house consultant working on a project basis. By now I was committed to gathering as much training and knowledge as possible to be able to achieve my dream. I developed my individual development plan which identified key areas of professional development and competencies that I wanted to build in my federal assignments. With my plan in mind, I participated in training and development programs in planning, interpersonal skills development, leadership, management, financial management, assessment, and other areas. These skills were necessary for my professional career and were also essential components for what I would later use to perform similar work in my practice.

For a number of family reasons I returned to Delaware from Washington. Midway through a rotational assignment I held in Philadelphia with the Environmental Protection Agency, I suffered a compound fracture of the ankle outside of work. This injury, with complications, required several surgical procedures and an extended period of recovery of over two years. The ankle injury affected my ability to commute back and forth to Philadelphia or Washington. I completed my final assignment in Philadelphia and declined a permanent appointment in Washington, DC.

I was faced once again with having to start over. I looked at my entrepreneurial desires and my skills and my dream of becoming an independent consultant. But as life would have it, the demands of the household and family were foremost, and there were great financial demands. While recovering from my ankle injury my mother suggested I continue my education, and pursue my creative skills in art. Specifically, she said, "Since you're flat on your back, you might as well use this time to get more in your head. Why not earn your Ph.D.? Maybe you should look at getting active with your artwork again? This may be God's way of slowing you down."

I knew that if I did get accepted into a doctoral program, I would be able to build the additional academic background and knowledge that I would need to practice as a management consultant. Inspired by my mother's comments and the confidence she had in me, I hobbled along on my crutches to the University of Delaware and told my academic advisor that I was interested in applying to the doctoral program in urban affairs and public policy. And great things began to happen! I was accepted into the program on a part-time basis.

Though not fully recovered, I began to seek employment again. I was offered a position in program research and evaluation involving state block grants and welfare programs. I functioned in the capacity of an in-house consultant working on strategic plans, management studies, and evaluations, and managing outside consulting contracts for larger projects.[2] Excited about actually working in the consulting-related work I envisioned, I decided that it was time to become certified in a training and assessment program to better understand human behavior in organizations and determine individual development needs. I saw an ad in the paper for management consultants' training for organizational consultants. It was as if this ad was speaking directly to me. I signed up for the two-day training in Philadelphia and became a certified consultant with the Carlson Learning Company in 1983.[3]

---

[2] While there, I also started a part-time business partnership venture with a colleague publishing children's books that targeted health, using African-American lead characters. The business, Tales N Tots Enterprises experienced modest success. I illustrated the three books the business produced and was responsible for new business development. The business was moderately successful and had distribution in local point of sale outlets. Through amicable agreement the company was dissolved in 1986 because of creative differences.

[3] Carlson Learning Companies was acquired and is now known as the Inscape Publishing Company. Goeins-Williams Associates, Inc. has had continuous affiliation and certification with the Inscape Publishing Network and company and is an authorized distributor of Inscape products.

Right around the same time that I got certified by the Carlson Learning Company I began to gather volunteer consulting experiences to develop my portfolio of work and client list. I was an active member of a number of community organizations, often on the boards of directors, and I looked for opportunities to solve problems. I submitted proposals to the boards to complete program evaluations, help with long-range planning, and facilitate retreats. On at least three occasions, the boards accepted my proposals and I successfully completed the work. I began to get involved in conducting management reviews, facilitating retreats, planning events, and assessing strengths of staff. Then I had a great opportunity to sign up as a management assistance consultant with the United Way of Delaware and to offer my skills and talents to help local organizations in their planning and evaluation needs. Two years after that then I obtained my first paid consulting job facilitating a strategic planning retreat for the board of directors of a local nonprofit organization.

I knew now that I was getting closer to my dream so I took another calculated risk. I left that planning and research position to accept an academic fellowship to complete my doctoral study at the University of Delaware. While at the University of Delaware I was able to design two specializations that fit exactly into the plan that I had for my business—social policy and analysis, and urban systems and planning. These were areas in which I needed further understanding, knowledge, and skills that would be important to have for my future consulting career.

I remember vividly the conversation I had with my dean about how earning my doctorate would give me the extra credential that I needed in order to achieve my ultimate dream which was to be an independent consultant in planning and evaluation with organizations. He admonished me and emphasized the fact that a Ph.D. was theoretical and for teaching, not for "applied work." I also told him my desire was to work with public as well as private organizations because I believed that one day that there would be need for consultants who could work in all sectors. Of course, he did not see my dream and tried to discourage me from taking this path. But I knew differently. I knew that I was working towards my dream. I could see the seed of my idea germinating and starting to sprout above the surface.

While completing my Ph.D. study, I continued to work as a professional management consultant. I wrote a business plan that clearly explained my business offering, annual sales, and marketing plan. In 1986, I established Goeins-Williams Associates by first searching for the name of my company in the handwritten record books in the basement of the county government archive office to prove that no other entity held my business name. (The system was not computer automated). Once I declared my business name unique, I was able to register the name of my company. I chose to use my name as the company name coupled with "Associates" because of its distinction and ambiguity. I was well aware of the fact that I was entering virgin territory as a woman-owned, minority-owned business and felt the name would give me greater credibility as well as present the image of the firm I wanted to grow into. Upon completing this requisite, I declared the Goeins-Williams Associates a business entity for the first time. I obtained my business license for professional services. From 1986 to 1989, I was well underway, with a successful part-time consulting practice while working full-time and completing my doctoral degree.

Nearing the end of my doctoral work I took another risk and applied for a competitive appointment as a legislative fellow for the Delaware General Assembly. I had an opportunity to select the committees I would staff in the House of Representatives and chose those that were in line with areas that I felt I needed growth and development: the Small Business and Economic Development, Land Use Planning and Transportation Committees. My work in the legislature lasted well beyond my appointment as major legislative issues on quality of life were debated and legislated. These issues, along with my interests and sudden death of the House Speaker, Brad Barnes, led to my continued work in the General Assembly as a consultant for the next several years.

I was starting to see the leaves sprout on my consulting practice and could see that I would be able to make a career out of the work. But I knew that I was still a novice and did not quite understand how to convert part-time consulting work into a full-time business. I had much to learn. I sought out the advice of two consultants in the area who were making a living at it.[4] I

---

[4] The late Pete Larsen was a successful planning consultant with the City of Wilmington. The late Ed Golin, a successful marketing consultant for area government and business agencies. Both gentlemen graciously granted interviews with me when I spoke with them about my

scheduled interviews with them and asked key questions about how to structure contracts, make a living as a consultant, and set fees. Both interviews proved invaluable and I never forgot what they explained to me.

> *You have to focus what you are offering, and clearly explain what you do so people will contract with you. They are buying you.*

The time I spent with them motivated me to begin to build my library of consulting book resources. I found that I spent a great deal of time in business sections of the bookstore gathering valuable resources on contracting and business management for the consultant.

For more than a year, a high level executive at the DuPont Corporation courted me to join the company as a mid-career executive. Impressed by my academic background and professional work in transportation policy and planning, the executive convinced me to take the opportunity with DuPont. Having an academic and professional orientation in the public sector it was not in my original plan to work with the private sector. But after careful consideration and soul-searching I believed that it was ordained that I take advantage of what I would learn. After all, I did not have corporate experience, which I would need to eventually become a full-time consultant. I also believed that if I took the road into a corporate career, I would become so comfortable with the income and benefits that I would never be able to find my way back to independence and entrepreneurship. But I took the chance—another risk—and it was worth it.

Off I went into the unknown to be an executive in a Fortune 500 company. For a while I thought that I had jumped ship—but when would I ever have this opportunity again? I trusted the executive who recruited me. Over time, he became a mentor, confidant, and friend. Initially, I was worried that I would lose my identity and the consultant practice and experience I built. To overcome this as I advanced my career at DuPont, I worked hard to have planned development opportunities that could be parlayed into business consulting. DuPont asked me to sign an agreement that I would not take on any consulting work while employed there. When clients continued to come to me to perform work as a consultant, to the extent that I was available I

---

desire to become an independent consultant. I am eternally grateful for the time they spent with me individually to answer my questions.

worked as a volunteer consultant. I had to go back to my old strategy of volunteer consulting to retain my active status and the possibility I would return to it again.

As it turned out, my career at DuPont lasted exactly five years, with 12 assignments with progressive responsibilities in planning, public policy, public relations, communications, leadership, and business management. Much of my work was very project-specific, similar to how I had functioned with the federal and state government. After my first year, I settled in to gather and build skills that I could use in my consulting practice. When I was employed with DuPont I was fully committed to my work there; however, with barriers to the advancement of women and minorities at that time and the instability of the corporation and threats of repeated downsizing, I saw that my vision of consulting was becoming a reality! I would obtain significant consulting experience in business that would give me the foundation for working in both the public and private sector. This was the vision I had communicated to my dean.

After my third year with DuPont, it became apparent that the constant movement I experienced was due both to imminent downsizing and the lack of future opportunity for a person with my background. I began to prepare my exit strategy to return to consulting, but not just part-time—full-time. During the fifth year, I worked at a fairly high level with a major business unit that was growing increasingly unstable and unprofitable.

I had just completed a major assignment in Chicago during which I worked exhaustively and saw little return for my efforts. It required me to spend a week away from my family and my office. At the airport, I learned my secretary had been fired by my boss and I had 175 voice mails! On the return flight, the plane was diverted to a different airport for a mechanical problem and I had an unplanned layover of eight hours. It was then and there that I had my *"Aha!* Moment." *I can do this,* I thought. *I can finally do this!* I composed my exit plan and the draft outline for my business plan in the airport that night. The time had come for me to form my exit strategy and look for an opportunity to leave the corporate world and start my consulting business again as a full time practice.

Shortly after this time, our business unit announced that it would make a major downsizing move because of the lack of profitability and poor business forecast. I saw this as my opportunity to seek a voluntary separation agreement with a "silver parachute." Before making my final decision, I sought advice and counsel from my mentors within the company. All encouraged me to volunteer for the early retirement to pursue my consulting career.

In October 1993, I voluntarily left employment with DuPont with a year of severance, full benefits, share options, retirement, a lump-sum payout and substantial savings in my 401K retirement fund. It was one of the best decisions I have made in my life. I still remember kicking my heels in the parking lot as I headed to my car on my last day of employment. I have never looked back.

Why Do You Really Want to be a Consultant?

As I have shared with you, I really wanted to be a consultant. Despite the complexity of weaving relevant professional and academic experience in preparation to work as a professional consultant, the reasons are quite simple.

- independence
- control over my own destiny
- high income potential
- the ability to fully use my skills, knowledge, abilities, and interests
- to build a legacy
- the opportunity to be an entrepreneur.

It is important for you to understand why you want to be a consultant so you can visualize where you are going. So much of the journey you take will rely on a clear vision of what you are trying to achieve as a consultant. You will need to work harder than most people to prepare yourself for the role and begin delivering the services you will offer. As you grow your business, it is vital that you have clarity of vision.

It may help to use this opportunity to capture your dream of becoming a consultant in the form of a personal vision statement. One way to do this is to go through this brief exercise. Close your eyes. Take some time to think about why you want to be a consultant. Answer these questions:

- What do I expect to gain?
- Why is consulting the career choice for me?
- Is being a consultant a part of my dream?
- How does becoming a consultant fit with how I see myself in the future?
- Why is it important that I become a consultant?

Write a concise sentence in response to each of these questions. After answering all the questions, you may want to take a further step and write a summary paragraph about what you've learned about yourself and your motivations for becoming a consultant. If you are already working as a consultant in some fashion, this exercise should help clarify why you are working in the field. If you take this exercise seriously you will have the beginning of a vision statement that will drive your planning as you become an intentional consultant.

3

TURNING THE DREAM INTO REALITY

Self-Assessment

In my introduction I wrote about the importance of being able to identify the unique niche for your consulting business. I also discussed the importance of being able to build credibility and trust with your clients and the fact that as a consultant you are selling *you*. As you grow your practice to possibly include other consultants you will be selling your firm and reputation. However, the reputation of your practice or your firm will still evolve from your credibility, trust, and niche focus that you establish early on. That niche focus is reliant upon the unique set of talents and skills, knowledge, and abilities that you alone possess.

By now you have already identified why consulting as a profession or career choice is important to you. Now, it is just as important to determine if you have what it takes—the range of skills and abilities and experiences—to create a viable consulting niche in the marketplace.

Before I left my corporate position I realized how important it was for me to narrow down my own skills, knowledge, talents, and abilities that would be essential to establishing an independent consulting business. As I have already shared with you in Chapter 1, I had many talents and skills, as well as abilities and interests, but not all of them would make sense as a potential offering of my consulting business. The challenge of identifying your own skill set of special knowledge and abilities may be even more difficult when you have a varied career background and multiple talents. One approach I took to address this dilemma was to invite other people to give me feedback in all of these areas. I recommend this as an exercise that you might want to undertake. I identified 100 people—colleagues, friends, mentors, business associates, clients—who worked with me in various contexts. I scheduled in-person meetings over a period of six months. I presented my vision of being a management consultant and stated some of the general areas that I thought I would offer, such as planning and program evaluation. I simply asked, *"Based on what you know about me, how do you see me interact with other people? What do you think are my strengths, areas of knowledge, special abilities, and talents? What work do you think people would be willing to hire me to perform as a consultant?"* I took excellent notes and recorded the conversations. I kept a journal of the interviews and summarized the information into key themes. It was very helpful in identifying potential offerings that I could include in my consulting business. Out of 100 interviews, seven or eight themes emerged: public relations; public speaking; strategic planning, organizational planning and improvement; working with people in organizations; evaluation; training; and meeting facilitation.

The key to becoming a successful consultant is having strong entrepreneurial skills, a willingness to take risks, and the ability to be flexible, creative, and innovative. You may find it valuable to assess your readiness to be an entrepreneur. There are a number of online assessments that allow you to examine this, such as one offered by the Centers for Ethics in Free Enterprise[5].

Finally, you might want to take your own skills inventory to determine your behavioral style. The DiSC behavioral style assessment[6] will give you direct feedback about your style preferences and what motivates you in certain environments. You may also want to look at some career-oriented assessments.

In my case, the self-assessment was affirming for me and provided a rich amount of information that was the basis for building business services that I

[5] Centers for Free Enterprise Entrepreneur Assessment: http://www.cefe.org/entrepreneur_survey.htm
[6] DiSC, is the acronym for Dominance, Influential, Steadiness and Conscientiousness, Assessment which can determine behavioral tendencies of individuals in response to work or social environments. DiSC assessments are available through authorized distributors of Inscape Publishing such as Goeins-Williams Associates. For more information visit:: www.goeinswilliams.com.

could offer. I recommend the self-assessment prior to putting together your initial business plan.

Business Planning

Now that you have determined your strengths, talents, abilities, skills, special areas of knowledge, and qualities that will make you a great consultant, you can begin developing your business plan. The business plan is your roadmap to determining your niche or focus, your offerings or what services you will provide, and how you will offer them to the marketplace (marketing).

Finding your niche and defining your focus

You can't possibly offer as a service everything that you are capable of doing. It's time to do some research. It was far easier for me to do this when I began my business, because management consultants were much rarer in the marketplace. Business consulting has grown as a profession, so finding a focus and developing a niche is more difficult, but necessary.

In my case, I initially wanted to focus primarily on public relations services to local government organizations. Because of my corporate experience, I had many contacts in public relations firms, and they seemed like a viable source for long-term sub-contracts. In researching my competition, I learned that, in my locale, the few firms offering public relations services were focusing on the communications services. I decided to select areas of public relations based on my competencies and determined that survey research, issues management, and lobbying were the best offerings to incorporate into my new business. I also found that there were other opportunities to evolve my business offerings in a combination that would be unique and have traction in the marketplace.

There are two essential aspects of this process. The first is to determine your *core competencies* from your self-assessment and then to conduct a competitor analysis. A *competitor analysis* is something you may want to do as you are developing your business plan and then, on a periodic basis, revisit as you hone your strategic plan. This analysis will provide you with a comprehensive view of the strengths and weaknesses of your current and future competitors to identify opportunities for and threats to your organization.[7]

---

[7] Bensoussan, Babette E. and Craig S. Fleisher Analysis without Paralysis: 10 Tools to Make

Develop a business plan

I speak to many business consultants and have found that the majority of them do not have business or strategic plans. I have also found that consultants with a business plan make more income, because they have a consulting practice, as opposed to simply being a contractor.

Although I had conceived the framework for my business plan in the airport that fateful day in 1993, I had to develop a more complete plan. My first business plan had the following elements:

1. Executive Summary
2. Market Plan
     a. Services
     b. Pricing Strategy
     c. Unique Offering
     d. Service Area
     e. Promotional Activity
3. Capability Statement
     a. Statement
     b. Resume of Principal
4. Client Consultation Summary
5. Cash Flow Analysis
6. Business Fact Sheet
     a. General Facts
     b. Business References

This first business plan required me to think through and commit to paper the essential elements of my business. I drew upon the interviews from my self-assessment and the core offerings I had created. I reviewed the competitor analysis and incorporated that into my market planning.

This process helped me to determine some critical issues related to my business operation such as the structure, business offering, pricing strategy, client prospecting plan, and financial plan, including my cash flow analysis. I determined that I would remain a sole proprietor until I hired my first employee. I incorporated my business in 1995. A semi-annual review was standard practice for my company and enabled me to made mid-course corrections that continued to improve the business and expand opportunities to focus the business and enhance revenues and reputation.

Every business should have a detailed business plan with a minimum of the elements that I listed. The research that you undertake is critical for laying the foundation for your business and helps to determine whether you are on or off course.

Determining fees

There are a number of ways to determine consulting fees. When I began my practice, I asked other consultants what their hourly or day rates were. I was also armed with information that I had from my assignment in Washington, DC, which gave me a better understanding of the day rates of experienced consultants. But Washington, DC, was not Delaware and the consultants that I met in Washington were with large firms and they were highly experienced. During my time with DuPont, I had worked extensively with suppliers who provided various services including public relations services and research—some of the services that I was providing. *But what should a new consultant charge on an hourly or daily basis?* I learned the hard way what fees not to charge!

My first year of full-time consulting I was desperate to obtain as much work as possible. I established different rates for non-profit, government and corporate clients. I began marketing my first training workshops and was not sure what to charge. My prospective client really liked my workshops and passed the information on to her superiors. They wanted to hire me! When asked about my fee I gave an extremely low rate. I thought that would guarantee they would hire me. Instead, it backfired. I was told confidentially that my fee was just so low that I must not know what I was doing and they chose someone else instead. I learned that the trainer they hired was paid five times more than what I had asked!

At that point I knew that I needed a better method to determine my fees. Here's what I've learned about determining fees from growing my practice:

- Quote work as an estimate and on a project basis, not on hourly or day rate, if possible.

- Clients respond to quality or value, not hourly rates.
- Consulting fees should be based on experience, the market rate (geographic influences) and knowledge, skills, abilities of the consultant (or team).
- Competitive bids should take into consideration real competition with other firms and bid fees and costs should bring a reasonable profit.

There are several ways to look at determining your fee when you begin your consulting practice full time. One way is to look at the total gross income you want to bring in on an annual basis and divide it by 12; that will provide you with your monthly income. Divide that total again by the estimated days you expect you can bill your clients and that will give you an approximate day rate. For the sake of argument, let's say that you would be able to bill out 15 days of work for clients on a monthly basis. Divide the day rate by 8 and that will determine your hourly rate. For example, if you want to gross \$100,000/year, using this method your day rate is \$555 and your hourly rate is \$69 as shown below:

Step 1.   \$100,000 /12 = \$8333

Step 2.   \$8333/15 = \$555

Step 3.   \$555/8 = \$69

Based on this scenario you may want to set an hourly rate of \$75.

Another way to determine your rate is to estimate the total number of hours you may be able to bill out each week. This can help you determine what hourly or day rate you want to charge your clients. For example, if you bill out three days a week based on your existing and projected client work, you can determine approximately how many days a month you will have income. Using this example, that would be 12 days. Twelve days a month for 12 months would be 144 days. How much is a reasonable fee? Five hundred dollars a day would generate a gross income of \$72,000. A day rate of \$1000 would generate \$144,000 in gross income.

The last method of determining your fee is to look at consulting surveys. Kennedy Consulting Research & Advisory[8] conducts an annual survey of consultants that includes a matrix of years of experience, industry, and hourly rates. This information gives a range of probable fees for the years of experience you have in the industry. Other professional organizations may conduct annual surveys. Inscape Publishing Network, of which our company is a member, conducts an annual survey of its members. Members have access to the survey data.

There are still other ways to determine your fee. Benchmarking is a way to see how your fees compare to others in your field. This is a method our company chose as part of our 10th Anniversary planning. We identified 10 consulting companies that were similar in size and offered some similar services. We were able to get their buy-in by offering to share the results of the survey with them. Based on our study we decided to increase our fees to slightly above the average fee and eliminate the differential rates for the different industry sectors we served.

Sometimes fees are determined by the contracts or after negotiation. The competitive bidding process may require you to bid lower fees in order to obtain the work. Some federal agencies such as the US Department of Justice have limits on the day rate they will pay consultants. You may determine that you will need to engage other consultants to assist you with work overflow. Your income will be determined by how well you are able to manage multiple projects and your ability to perform the work that pays your highest billable rate.. When negotiating fees, you must determine before the negotiation process how low you will go. Experience has taught me that fee integrity is essential. Your fee should be reasonable and still allow you to make a profit. If you give away your work, the referrals you generate may be future clients with expectations of lower fees.

Strategic planning

A strategic plan is part of a toolkit that all consultants should have to help their businesses grow. I operated my business for three years before we undertook a strategic planning process. By the end of our third year, I had moved my business out of my home, took on leased office space closer to current and prospective clients and hired a few full- and part-time staff.

---

[8] Kennedy Consulting Research & Advisory, www.kennedyinfo.com

Before I took my own company through this process, I was like the cobbler whose kids did not have shoes. After all, facilitating strategic planning is one of our core services and work I cut my teeth on. I knew that it was something vital for us to do, but it required a major effort to begin the process. But the effort was well worth our while. When our company developed our first strategic plan, we were able to increase our gross revenues by 140% the following year.

A strategic plan is different from a business plan because it uses an environmental scanning process that is more sensitive to trends, political issues, and economic cycles. By following the strategic planning process, consultants can move from sole proprietorships to consulting practices. The strategic planning process will enable you to clarify your vision, mission, and values. Conducting a Strengths, Weakness, Opportunities, and Threats (SWOT) analysis will enable you to determine your strengths, weaknesses, opportunities, and threats to your business. The strategic planning process enables you to identify critical issues and develop strategic goals and a tactical plan to help you achieve your vision and meet profit objectives.

What is most important about the strategic planning process is the feedback that you solicit from clients and a review of your own metrics to gauge your performance. For example, if one of your strategic objectives is to achieve 100% satisfaction of your clients, then an annual survey is one of the tactics you would employ to determine your actual performance. The questions you develop for your client survey should yield specific information about your services and performance that allows you to pinpoint continuous improvement initiatives. This, in turn, is what enables you to grow your business.

A business plan is still important but it is more static. Both plans are equally important but have different purposes. The key is to have both and regularly assess your plans on a semi-annual basis.

Turning Contacts to Contracts

Your business plan is great but it won't get you your first client. Your brochure looks great, too, but it won't get you your first client. Neither will your website or your business card. What will get you a contract and repeated work are your contacts, your network, and building an outstanding reputation.

As I wrote in Chapter 1, I built my beginning client list through volunteer consulting which helped to build referrals for paid work. About 70–80% of our business is through referrals from satisfied clients. This is a metric that we monitor through our strategic planning process.

I explained how I interviewed 100 people about my prospective business services and asked for feedback. During the course of my interview, I also asked if they would consider hiring me to perform work for them. Out of this initial group, I was able to obtain five retainer contracts! Two weeks after I left my corporate position I had contracted work at the day rate I showed in my business plan. Two of these contracts lasted for three years. Just from the exercise of identifying key contacts and spending time with them about my business, I was able to generate stable contracts. This was a 5% rate. We have tracked this metric for our business and found that we have a contact to contract rate now of about 80%.

My first major contacts were with people that I developed significant or trusted business and professional relationships. Of course, I was using a Rolodex then and methods of developing relationships and contacts has changed monumentally since then with the advent of social media. Social media has become a game changer by easing the ability to connect with people. Social media used well can multiply contacts in a more efficient manner. At the same time, without a clear social media plan, using it can backfire. Consultants should focus on building quality relationships and trust. There is really no substitute for face to face meetings to generate trust, the foundation for consulting relationships.

Credentials—Professional Affiliations, Certifications

Credentials are vital for consultants and there are many ways to obtain them to add perceived value to what you do. Credentials can include professional affiliations, designations, earned academic degrees, and business certifications and memberships. Credentials provide a way to fill the trust gap for consultants. Accruing credentials is a vehicle for development, building a professional network and referral system, and obtaining contracts. Keep in mind that a large number of referrals come from other consultants.

As a business consultant you will want to have access to other consultants whom you can recommend to your clients for work that is complementary to your focus but not directly what you offer. For example, our company offers some traditional public relations consulting such as moderating focus groups, but we do not work directly in communications. We have several consultants that we can confidently recommend to clients in this area.

Clients look for credentials to determine qualifications of consultants they choose to hire. Credentials also contribute to your individual and company reputation and image. Certifications can attest to your company's capability.

Gaining academic credentials—such as advanced degrees and specializations—is one such method. Academic degrees are good but probably not enough. Having a Ph.D. in a field unrelated to the consulting work you may offer may have little value to clients. Community colleges and the continuing education arms of colleges and universities offer short-term certification programs that build your credentials and prepare you to be better suited to carry out the work you perform. Credentials should be related to the business plan and the services you offer.

When I started my business I had completed my master's in public administration and I promoted my specialization in agency management as a way to bridge the trust gap with new clients. I also obtained certifications in administration of training programs like DiSC through the former Carlson Learning Company. I became an approved member of the Institute for Management Consultants (IMC) which has a professional designation for management consultants.[9] The IMC offers a rigorous training program and requires recommendations from paying clients in consideration for the certified management consultant (CMC) designation. This certification is a tremendous option for a consulting professional who desires additional certification.

---

[9] Institute for Management Consultants, USA is a professional association for management consultants www.imcusa.com

There are many other options for consultants and it depends on the field of work or your focus. For example, if you are an executive coach or facilitator, there are professional organizations that offer recognized certification programs. If you are a consultant or trainer who is also a motivational speaker, approved membership in the National Speaking Association (NSA) is a wonderful option. Approved memberships in professional organizations require that you meet a minimum standard to gain entry into the organization, such as a minimum number of paid engagements, competencies, or references.

Memberships in approved organizations and other professional and business associations like the National Federation of Independent Businesses, or the National Association of Women Business Owners, and the American Society of Training and Development have local chapters, networking and educational events, and opportunities to become active in leadership. Local and state chambers of commerce provide similar opportunities. Your decisions about your professional affiliations should be in alignment with your business and strategic plans.

- What relationships do you need to cultivate?
- What industry sectors are most important to your current and future business?
- How much time do you have to attend meetings and participate in what is offered?
- Does the offering of the association fit with your ability to take full advantage of it?

These programs and groups add to your ongoing professional development and also provide you with a ready network of likeminded colleagues who can offer support, help you solve business problems, and serve as a source of referrals. These programs also help with the problem of isolation so many new consultants experience—especially since most begin as solo-entrepreneurs.

As you develop your business you will identify emerging needs in the marketplace that may cause you to consider seeking professional development and/or obtaining new credentials. It is an ongoing process and is never static if you want to grow your business.

Certifications for your business can be helpful but also confusing. There are a number of certifications that you may want to consider but it depends on what kind of consulting business you have. Are you a business-to-business consultant or a business-to-consumer consultant? Are you seeking contracts with the federal, state, or local government? Do you want to work with corporations?

Third-party certifications can help grow your business. If you are a minority- or woman-owned business you should consider certification, because without them, you may actually lose opportunities. While I have always had some reservation about minority business designations, the fact is that there is a compelling reason for doing so.

Many state and local governments have aggressive programs in place to use Minorities, Women, Business Enterprises (MWBEs) because of the historical poor record of contracting with these firms. Because of the potential revenue savings for governments to get the best deal, there is added pressure to work with MWBEs that are local and can often provide the best value. If you are not designated, clients will not be able to find you. In general, consulting, which falls in the professional services category, is a catch all for every service from architectural and engineering services to accounting and training. Having a certification will give your firm an opportunity to be found in a directory with the specific services that you offer.

National organizations like the National Minority Supplier Diversity Council and National Women Business Owners Corporation provide certification that is recognized by corporations who prefer to work with certified suppliers. Corporations who are recipients of federal contracts are also under pressure to do business with qualified minority- and women-owned suppliers. Our company at one point had memberships with five professional business associations, a regional, and two national certifications. Ongoing certifications and memberships should be directly related to your strategic plan. Will these certifications lead to increased revenues for targeted clients? If not, then perhaps this certification is one to skip.

4

EVOLVING YOUR BRAND

The intentional consultant must ask the following questions, and many more, on an initial and ongoing basis.

- Who are you?
- What is your business?
- What do you have to offer?
- Why would anyone hire you as a consultant?
- Who are your clients?
- Why do they come to you?
- What makes them come back to you?
- What is your value in the marketplace?

The Marketing Plan

The marketing plan is the foundation for your business because it clarifies your service strategies, your key messages, your promotional and client plans. Without a well-developed marketing plan, you are not an intentional consultant but someone who is functioning from contract to contract. The marketing plan should tie into your business and strategic plan. It is a framework, and it should be flexible to respond to marketplace changes and transitions.

As with the other plans you will need to have for your business, I caution you to not become overwhelmed by the planning process. The biggest problem that I see holding back other business consultants is that, because the planning process seems overwhelming, they decide not to have plans at all and go with their intuition in promoting their business. This causes an alignment problem because marketing materials are not developed with clear messages about the business and the consultant.

My recommendation is to start with a simple marketing plan that teases out some of the basic marketing concepts that you will need to clarify; as your business develops and evolves, your marketing plan can evolve accordingly.

Here are the elements that I have used as a basis for my marketing plan:

1. Services
   a. What services do you offer and to whom?
   b. Are your services segmented by industry?
2. Pricing
   a. How much do your charge for your services?
   b. What is the rationale for your fee structure?
3. Unique Position in the Marketplace
   a. Why is your consulting practice unique?
   b. What do you offer that separates you from the competition?
   c. How will you deliver your work?
4. Promotions
   a. What is your general promotional plan to lure business prospects?
   b. How will you promote yourself as an expert? Your business?
   c. What marketing methods and materials will you use and how?
   d. What is your plan for referrals and repeat business?
   e. What plans do you have for paid advertising, sponsorships, or charitable giving?
5. Key Messages
   a. What are the key strengths of your business?
   b. What is your value to the client?
   c. What are the "top of mind" thoughts that you want clients to have about your business?

A comprehensive marketing plan will be useful in shaping all of your marketing activity and directing traffic to your business. Essentials today are a company website and business cards. Over the years we have seen less emphasis on paper marketing (brochures, business cards, presentation materials) and more emphasis on technology (websites, social media, etc.)

You will need to develop collateral materials that come from your marketing plan. You will want to incorporate key messages and tag lines, for example, in all of your material. For example I have found it useful to develop a capability statement and PowerPoint slide show about our business and an email brochure.

Become an expert

Key to your promotional strategy is becoming known as an expert in your niche, but most beginning consultants have limited resources to dedicate to marketing.

One of the most effective marketing tools is to speak as a subject matter expert at conferences. Most of the time you will not be paid for your presentation, and you may have to pay for all of your travel expenses. However, the promotional value will be tremendous. You will have the power of online presence and links to promotional materials of national, regional, and local organizations, and recorded presentations that you may be able to use to promote your expertise. Over time these presentations can increase your popularity, lead to referrals, and have residual value that will cause people to connect to your website or your name. It is a critical aspect of building your company's name and your individual expertise. To increase expertise of your team, employees and associates should participate as well.

Agreeing to speak on webinars or at conferences, and arranging the promotion so the asking party does the work is most effective. I once developed a seminar series for a downtown university training center. We agreed on a 50:50 split on costs for the workshops. The university mailed the brochure to a mailing list of over 6000 people in the region. Even though the workshops were not a great success because of low participation and the eventual closing of the location, the brochures brought me new business. One lead came from a senior vice president of a regional hospital who received the brochure in the mail. I was invited to develop a program for the hospital that had been featured in the brochure. That was the start of a relationship with the hospital that lasted more than five years. We provided assessment, consulting, and training on numerous projects for many of its business units.

Writing articles for publication can establish you and your business as a subject matter expert as well. The first few years I was in business, writing articles was a key component of my marketing plan and I worked to submit articles on a periodic basis to business and trade periodicals. Publication of these articles helped to position me as an expert on key topics related to my business and generated inquiries from reporters who sought me for advice on these topics for business and the broader community.

Build relationships with the media and cultivate your contacts. One of your promotional strategies should include issuing regular press releases to the local, regional, and national media that positions you and your company as experts in your core areas. Press releases can be written to promote new services, awards, publications, presentations at conferences, associate news, anniversaries, and other newsworthy items. You may also want to create news by inviting the media to attend key events that you host. Following up with news reporters who quote you or publish your articles with handwritten thank you notes will guarantee that they will contact you again.

Giving back to the community

Pro bono activities also can fit as part of your community outreach strategy. I believe that all consultants should have a community program which also incorporates your charitable giving strategy. As your business grows, you, as an intentional consultant, will have a chance to support causes that are consistent with your personal values. Deciding on the causes you will support will give you a way to focus your pro bono activity and giving strategy. Our focused giving strategy is geared toward senior citizens, education, and mentoring programs.

Your community outreach program is a positive way to become involved at the community level in something that you care about, establish goodwill in the community and, at the same time, promote your business. The volunteer work that you choose, the community and business boards on which you serve, should be part of your marketing strategy in how you position yourself, your image, and your business.

Branding

You are branding your business by everything you do that defines who and what your company is in the eyes of the public and your clients. Protecting your brand and image is of utmost importance, because it is your brand that gives value to your company.

Building your brand means developing a positive image and positioning your business expertise and yourself. Your corporate values, beliefs, and principles should be developed by you and your employees when you create your strategic plan. When you live the values in your business, over time these values will be realized in the perceptions others hold about you and your company. If your behavior, or that of your employees or associates, is outside the set of values you establish and promote for your company, you run the risk of doing damage to your reputation and image.

For example, one of our company's values is to maintain the highest degree of ethics and integrity in our research when working with our clients. On more than one occasion, we have had clients ask us to modify our focus group research findings because they did not like what we learned about how consumers viewed them. We never honor such requests, even when the client pushes back with threats. Word got out once when we refused to compromise our research; we later heard from other clients through referrals that "Goeins-Williams Associates will not soft-pedal research findings. You might not like what you hear, but you will always get honest results." We have also "fired" a client who has not acted in an ethical way.

How do you determine your brand? You may think you can describe it, but the best way to go about this is to ask your clients with a brief survey:

1. What is the general feeling they have about your company?
2. How do you describe the brand?
3. Would you refer us or our company to another organization? To a friend? Why?

Getting and Keeping Clients

Our knowledge-based global economy has helped to fuel competition. Businesses that survive in this economy do so because of the strength of the relationships they build with existing and new clients. I recently talked to a longtime client who has continued to hire our firm as he has transitioned through several organizations. I asked him why he keeps coming back to us. He told me the key was the quality of our relationship and the trust he had built with our firm over the years. More than half of our business is with repeat clients and about 60% of new business is from referrals from satisfied clients.

Creating a client philosophy

Clients are your most vital asset. Without clients you will not have a business. When you nurture your client relationships you can build repeat business and referrals. My philosophy is, "The client is always right, even when they are wrong." When you are a consultant you cannot lose sight of the fact that your client is your client. You are always working to ensure that your services and products exceed their expectations.

Do you have a client philosophy? Our client philosophy is embedded in our client plan which is an extension of our marketing plan. If you do not have a client philosophy, it is time to develop one. Here are a few questions to get you started on developing a written client philosophy and plan.

- How do you treat your client?
- How do you approach clients?
- How do you welcome them into your business?
- How do you reward loyal clients?
- How do you thank them for their business?
- How do you keep in touch with your clients?

Once you commit your philosophy to writing, you will need to ensure that it is clearly communicated and understood by your staff and associates who speak for your company. You must practice what you preach, and so must they.

Building trust builds business

Building trust with your clients comes from effective communication, consistent performance, and exceeding their expectations. Many of our long-term clients have become friends over the years. That does not happen by accident, but by building strong relationships. Your client philosophy provides guidance to you about relationship-building. Thinking beyond the client relationship means nurturing it. *Who is your client? What do they like? What are they about?*

Getting to know your clients personally gives you insight into how you will need to work with them so you can anticipate their wants and needs. Understanding their behavioral style, their personal interests, their individual and professional development goals will allow you to tailor your services to meet their needs. Our company has developed an ability to refer our clients to each other because of the unique work that we offer. This is an aspect of our business that our clients have grown to value about the relationship we have with them. We have maintained the records of our clients dating back over twenty years. For clients who repeat strategic planning on a cycle basis, this is especially important; we may only service them every five years. They will say to us, "That's why we come back to you—we know you will have our files and you know us."

My dear late associate gave me this line—*Dance with the one who brought you.* It simply means to remember who brought you to the party. I believe that maintaining relationships with long time clients is a way to do this. Reach back to old and loyal clients often. Dance with your client by being in step, anticipating needs, and being a partner.

Listening to clients builds trust. Meet with clients initially to determine the full extent of their needs, asking questions and clarifying client objectives. Asking questions at critical milestones during a project or after the completion of work will facilitate open communications and build trust. Be proactive and consistent with your clients. When you discover a problem, solve it promptly. I once gave a full refund for a meeting that was facilitated by one of my employees because my client was unhappy with the outcome. On principle, I could have offered to give her a partial refund—perhaps half of the cost because some work was performed. But to preserve the relationship, I refunded the total fee and still paid my employee. I practiced the philosophy that our client is always right. Some 15 years later I still have a firm relationship with this client.

Exceeding expectations

My experience has taught me that a clearly stated scope of work outlined in the contract or agreement provides the fundamentals for good client relations. Your scope of work is what you commit to do for your fee. That means that the clarity will ensure that you can meet the requirements of your contract. The initial meeting upon contract signing is essential for developing a shared understanding of how you will complete the work and the guarantee of support you will get from the client. A lack of a clear scope of work can result in "scope creep" and unclear expectations about what you will do. Once you move into a gray area and have to tell a client that you cannot perform work they expect you to do, then you disappoint them.

When you have a team it is important that everyone shares an understanding of the requirements of a contract to avoid "scope creep." In one of our strategic planning retreats, my team and I discussed the importance of clearly communicating expectations with clients at the onset of the contracts. We had noticed that we were performing more and more work outside of the scope of the contract. Under pressure to exceed expectations, we found ourselves doing this more often than not. We determined, however, that we could still be respectful of our clients and use requests for more work as an opportunity to ask our clients for contract amendments for additional work. We also role-played with each other on how to handle such requests. While away at a conference shortly thereafter, I found a hanging monkey novelty toy that had Velcro sticky tape on his hands. I brought the monkey to the office and we nicknamed him *Scope Creep*. He became a mascot that would find himself moving form office to office of the team member who became involved in a scope creep activity. Sometimes for fun the mascot was thrown down the stairs or found his way in the drawer of an associate.

It should be noted that there are times when you will do more than is asked by your client. In fact, I have built my business on exceeding expectations and doing more than is asked. Most times excess work is planned; however, there is always unforeseen work that comes along with project work. It is always our business commitment to deliver 100% quality. Experienced consultants learn that, when it is a new client or less familiar work, it always takes longer than estimated to complete a job. That knowledge can be factored into any proposal.

Client analytics

Analyzing your client database is a great way to learn more about your clients. At a minimum, you need to know who your typical client is and how they find you. Surveying your clients will give you more information about their preferences and feedback about your service. It is also essential to know what they like or don't like about your business and what they know about it.

We have developed a client intake form to gather information on the front end about our clients. The information captured includes how the client learned about our services and products and referrals. It also captures specifications of the request and follow up requirements from the inquiry. This data gleaned from the intake form gives us valuable information about what marketing campaigns and promotions are most successful, where referrals come from, the months of the year that tend to be more active. We are also able to segment the requests by industry. Repeat clients and loyal clients who give referrals are rewarded with special discounts, gifts, preferred rates, or tickets to attend special client events. We love our clients and we show them!

Every client has a monetary value of costs to your business including: marketing your brand, public relations, and promotions. The costs of obtaining a new client is up to five times of the cost of keeping a client.[10] Cultivating existing client relationships allows you to build your brand, client loyalty, referral networks, and friendships.

We implement a number of strategies to cultivate our preferred client base. My favorite is the use of the "Ideal Client" worksheet which we have developed to analyze projects after the work is completed. This is our own rating system based on what we believe is our ideal client. For example, one attribute we rate on this form is the working relationship and client support. The form, which is scaled on a 1–5 (high to low) rating scale, allows us to assign a numeric rating to our clients. Sometimes the costs of keeping a client is greater than the cost of getting a new one. We use this system to eliminate the "duds" and spend more time cultivating repeat work with our "stars."

---

[10] Timm, Paul R. Seven Power Strategies for Building Customer Loyalty Performance Improvement Council, Incentive Marketing Association, Customer Retention: Keeping your best customers for the long run.

Sometimes having the wrong clients brings you bad future business. Cultivate clients that give you referrals for work that generates the highest profit margins and consistent work. Use your ranking system to rate your clients (1, 2 , 3, 4, and 5, for example). Then evaluate your client list. Does your client base reflect your strategic direction? How can you cultivate more 1s and 2s and eliminate the 5s?

Survey your clients after they purchase products or use your services. We created a survey a number of years ago to give to our clients upon completion of a project or purchase. I have learned over the years to give the survey to the client in person and wait for it to be completed. We compile the results of the returned surveys on an annual basis. We have learned what our clients value most about our company, and they learn more about us, too. The survey also lists all of our business offerings; there are always services they are unaware we offer.

On a larger scale, it helps to inform your business of broader strategic initiatives that may be helpful in narrowing or redefining certain services or products. On an individual basis, you can use the survey as a tool for follow-up and provide your capability information, the link to your website, a personal note, or a product sample. This is a great way to determine strategies to educate your client.

It is your responsibility to educate your clients. Once you find what they do not know about your business, it is up to you to inform them. There are many ways to do this from e-newsletters to trade shows and social media. But the most effective way still is to pick up the phone and ask for time to meet and brief your client on services they may not be familiar with. We reach out to our clients to schedule time to meet and bring them up to date on our services and products. Every time we have done this it has resulted in new business or a referral.

When you provide the highest quality service to your clients, listen to them, solve their problems and consistently meet their needs, they will recognize the value you provide. Clients who recognize your value will not be focused on price.

5

MINDING YOUR BUSINESS

Business Operations

Running any business contains three elements: running your business; managing your business, and developing future business. Independent consultants may be challenged more than other small businesses because very often, they are the business. I find myself always working on these three elements. A good strategic plan can help to guide your focus to what you will do in each one of these areas on a year-to-year basis.

When I began my consulting as an independent freelance service, I clearly remember that in my first year my focus was on replacing the salary that I earned in my previous corporate position. I was living under threat that I needed to make at least what I earned at my previous employment to be a viable consultant. I did not really think of myself as a business, even though I had my business name. I thought of myself as a freelance independent individual consultant. Somewhere between my second and third year in business I recognized that I needed to focus on the business entity that I created, not just me as an individual. I needed to begin building the company brand, with me as its leader and principal consultant.

As a startup business, my key partners were my certified public accountant and my business counselor at the Small Business Development Center. These individuals had been resources since I formally established my business entity in 1986. With the counsel of my CPA and business advisor, I made what I believe were appropriate moves to grow my business.

To maximize my income, I needed to develop the business operation of the company and have the mindset of the company, which was far different than having a mindset of a freelance consultant. I even took on a motto to help drive the new direction: "Be small, feel big." When you begin to see yourself as operating a firm or a practice as opposed to an independent freelance individual consultancy, many things can change from there.

In my third year, I hired my first staff and began to see larger contracts. I changed my Internal Revenue Service (IRS) tax filing status from sole proprietor to corporation, because my income was increasing and I had greater exposure to associated risks. When I incorporated I named myself as president and CEO and appointed an executive vice president. I also took on the role of secretary for my business and tax purposes. I began to look at expanding my company's possibilities and leveraging our work by talking with other consultants who might make a potential fit for joint ventures or as associates. I knew that if I could expand beyond just me, I would be able to leverage my singular efforts and seek larger contracts.

One of the challenges I experienced the first two to three years in business was the ability to stabilize cash flow. I did not know how to project uncertain income into the future. In my initial business plan, I projected establishing subcontracting relationships with public relations firms in the tri-state area. I was able to obtain several of these lasting from two to five years. These contracts presented steady income; however, they generally paid in 90 to 120 days after billing. This would have been a real financial disaster if I did not plan and receive income from other sources.

Other consultants have often asked me, "How did you sustain yourself the first year of business? How do you get to the point where you are able to predict what your monthly income will be so that you can pay your bills? How do you to get to the position where you can actually hire staff?"

I learned in my first few years of business that when you are looking at your budget, you have to remember that you have to create a budget with two parts, income and expense. You have to manage both.

Early in my first year, I developed five contracts (for 1–3 years) to perform project-specific work set up as retainer arrangements with a set amount of monthly income based on an agreed-upon scope of work. Another strategy that worked well was to obtain subcontracts, also on a retainer basis, with major firms in the tri-state area. These contracts tended to be on a year-to-year basis, but I was fortunate enough to hold several of these and I was able to estimate what my monthly income would be from the subcontracts. The subcontracts were a combination of bid and no-bid agreements.

I was able to become reengaged with the Carlson Learning Network which was a multilevel company at the time. I found that the Carlson Learning company and their educational products such as DiSC, were highly aligned with my business offerings in professional and organizational development. I had experienced some modest success as part of the multilevel nature of this business and earned sufficient commissions for an extended period. Commissions were a function of sales and as the training and development aspect of our company grew and we incorporated the products into our training, the sales and commission income grew as well, which added to our bottom line.

Business people sometimes lose sight of the expense side of the budget. Professional services consultants are in a position to generally enjoy higher profit margins than other businesses because overhead costs tend to be lower. But as you move into a realm of hiring employees, obtaining office space, and incurring other fixed expenses your income may rise because of increased capacity but your margins may shrink. According to *Best Firms to Work For 2008* survey by *Consulting* Magazine, consultants at small and medium-sized firms spent only 70% of their time on client engagements and business development, and they spent 30% on administrative functions compared to larger sized firms who spent 80% of their time on client engagements and business development and 20% on administrative functions.

The fixed part of the budget includes, of course, all of your operating expenses: salary, loans, interest expenses, taxes, bank and credit card fees, business licenses. memberships, insurance, marketing and promotional materials and activities, automobile, secretarial expense, computer and e-commerce expense, supplies, printing, accounting fees, professional services, utility costs (phones, cable, Internet service, electric, gas, security). To the extent that you can control these fees and manage these costs you will increase your profitability.

Every year that I have been in business my annual budget changes, so it is important to not only have an annual budget when you're working on a day-to-day basis but to project your budget for the coming year. I like to begin my budget planning for the coming year about six months prior to the end of the current year. The budget forecast includes projected income from retainer contracts as well as looking at trends I see in current spending and in the history of the business. It also projects income from product sales and factors in environmental influences identified in the strategic planning process that may influence the direction of the business. Over the years, I have been able to forecast anywhere from 60% to 90% of the revenue for the coming year by the third quarter of the current year. I am always looking at ways to reduce fixed expenses. In the fourth quarter, I generally approach clients about purchasing products or pre-ordering at a discounted rate for the coming year. This strategy works because businesses may be seeking ways to reduce their tax liability before the end of the calendar year.

These budget management strategies enabled me to move from a home-based business after three years to a leased space (closer to my clients) and on to owning a commercial office buildings and to evolve from a sole proprietor to a CEO employing a team of associates and a small staff.

Remember, as an individual consultant you are only one person. *Be small, look big.* In other words, look for ways to expand your capacity to manage your business operations so you can focus on actually performing the work that brings in revenue. One method I discovered to manage operations more efficiently was to think about all of the major operations functions as separate departments. For example, the accounting function requires a certified public accountant and a bookkeeper. It also requires administrative staff to manage the regular upkeep and maintenance of our accounts.

Another department is marketing, which includes all of the public relations activities, advertising, promotion, press releases, special events planning. There are times when you will need to bring in outside resources to help you carry out your marketing activities. Of course, this function requires its own plan. In our case, I have taken on much of the marketing responsibility myself, but also delegated aspects of our "marketing department" to other staff. I've also hired contractors to carry out various aspects of the marketing plan such as designing logos, preparing brochures, developing and maintaining websites, designing products, etc. The key for any business operation is to know when it costs more to do that work yourself—because you don't have either the expertise or the time—then contract the service to be provided outside of your company. That may mean that some of the things you would like to do, you simply cannot afford until you have the income to cover the expense.

Another department is human resources. I found that as our company began to grow, it was necessary to take on many of the tasks of a larger employer with regard to human resources management. That means developing an employee handbook, benefits administration, policies, interview practices, hiring protocol, career development and training opportunities for staff, and performance evaluation. Again, I took on developing the primary aspects of this "department," but I also learned that there were certain areas that required expertise beyond mine. In this case, it meant taking on legal insurance to cover some liability associated with hiring employees, and attending seminars and conferences to ensure that our practices were up to standard.

Once we owned property, it became clear our company needed a buildings or facilities management department. Management and maintenance of facilities, including leases, property maintenance, security and safety, property taxes, moving, furniture and fixtures, managing systems so that utilities function efficiently and safely, are aspects of the business that, if not functioning properly, can shut a business down. During the 22 years that I have been in business, we have acquired lease property, commercial office buildings and commercial mortgages, leased out properties on a regular basis to other businesses, and sold properties. Much of this work was beyond my capacity and expertise and I sought support from my executive vice president to handle the contracts, and hired lawyers and real estate brokers.

As you grow, the intentional consultant must think with an eye to the future and be mindful of capacity. Use your own resources to generate revenues through contract performance. As you increase employees and associates who will perform work for your company, always protect your brand. Hire experts to do the work you cannot do because of lack of time or expertise. Always hire outside if what you are paying is less than what you charge someone else for you to do the work.

Managing Projects and Deliverables

Tracking your work will enable you to predict schedule demands and business cycles. For example, we know the business cycles of each of our lines of service. We know when our clients tend to order products, the busiest times of the year for training, the busiest times of the year for strategic planning, and when our clients are likely to want to begin comprehensive organizational assessments. Tracking the work that you perform, contracts by type of service provided, looking at your client data, and conducting end-of-the-year reviews will help you more efficiently execute the work that you do.

QuickBooks Pro has excellent resources for looking at client data, profitability, and other financial performance analyses. You should get into the habit of pulling all of your financial statements on a quarterly basis at least, conducting budget comparisons of previous years, and looking at other reports, such as profit by job, for overall profitability.

The point is that you have to figure out how to minimize the time you spend on business operations so that you can do the work that brings revenue into your company. Sometimes you can get so busy doing the work that you lose sight of an important business operation requirement. That's why it is so important to have clear plans with performance measures and timed objectives and tactics.

Every consultant should know how to manage projects. Consultants who are able to build a practice learn how to manage multiple projects. I've known consultants who work on one contract at a time, complete that work, and then look for the next project. That type of approach will not generate sufficient cash flow to sustain an individual consultant let alone a practice or company. So how does one manage multiple contracts as just one consultant? I'd like to share with you some ideas that have worked for me.

First of all, we keep track of all the requests for work, as I stated earlier, using a client intake form. I follow up those requests and keep them in a pending folder until we move forward with that work. Second, we track proposals that have been submitted on a project management form we have created which specifies basic proposal information, proposal submission date, and expected date of notification of selection. These project forms track solicited competitive bid proposals. The third type of project we track are active projects. Information tracked on a monthly basis includes: the nature of the work, the major deliverables and dates required, and the end date of the contract. This data is aggregated on a monthly and annual basis and entered into Excel spreadsheets.

The project summary form gives us a way to look at the status of all active projects and deliverables schedule on a weekly and monthly basis. By updating this on a monthly basis we are able to keep track of our work and ensure that none of the work falls through the cracks. As principal, this information helps me to track assignments and manage capacity and, to some extent, cash flow.

Individual projects are managed by the consultant who is assigned to do that work. Consulting associates are held accountable for meeting their deadlines and delivering quality drafts for review. We manage project deliverables by weekly progress meetings and frequent reports to clients per the scope of work. Again, working in alignment with a clear, comprehensive scope of work minimizes the chances of falling through the cracks and not delivering what is intended.

New Business Development

New business development is probably one of the most challenging aspects of business for consultants.

- How do you network?
- To whom do you give your card?
- What trade shows really bring in business for your company?
- How do you generate quality leads?
- How do you ensure that the time you spend in business development brings you a client?

All these questions are important, especially in today's economy.

Early in my business, I used any downtime to focus on marketing and professional development. During my first two years in business, the summers were fairly light so I used that time to focus on strategic planning, writing articles and press releases and developing new products. In the startup phase, my primary method of obtaining new business was through developing and selectively distributing presentation folders and capability statements and getting that information before prospective clients who I thought would be interested in using my services. Speaking at conferences and presenting workshops at trade shows and professional conferences was another way that I was able to generate interest. Trade shows, although costly because of preparation, registration fees, and travel expenses, may generate future business leads as well as product sales.

Our best tool for new business development has been a consistency of high quality performance that generates referrals. Quite often our business referrals will come to us with several recommendations to contract with our firm for the work they need. We have had a website since 1995 and it consistently serves as a resource for our clients, generates leads, and sells products. Our ability to generate new work has increased every year that we have had a website. Social media does play a part in new business development and although we are not experts in this area we have seen some contracts come to us through this source. The bottom line is that today's consultant must be adept in every form of business promotion to develop new business. Each medium is different and requires different tactics. It may be necessary to contract with another professional to perform this work if you do not have the capability in-house.

The intentional consultant develops a plan for business development that is based on strategic opportunities identified in the strategic plan. Over the last eight years in particular, our company has been able to identify economic growth sectors to target our offerings. We are now working in areas that we projected five years ago would continue to bring in revenues.

When you are a sole proprietor, new business development is something you have to do on a regular basis and you must be very disciplined about it. That means identifying prospective clients and contacting them by phone or e-mail and following up on a regular and consistent basis. Technology has reduced many barriers to entry for new business consultants, so competition has grown in intensity. Intentional consultants who use a personal touch may be more distinctive.

As your company grows, this is something that someone else can do for you. In our company, the Executive Vice President has the role of new business development and works to develop and manage the plan of contacting clients, following trends in the marketplace, and making connections with prospective clients. New business development does not work without a strategy. Sometimes that means just being seen, just getting out of the office. That is very challenging for consultants who are busy managing their business and performing contracted work for the business. But if you lose sight of this, you could lose your business and you may not be able to sustain your business or your company.

Finding the Right People

There are many different kinds of people you need for your consulting business. You will form alliances with other consultants to create joint ventures or offer referrals. You will need to hire professionals to perform the work that is not cost effective for you to perform yourself. As you grow your business, hiring employees or bringing on associates are options that may increase revenues. Vendors and suppliers are sometimes extensions of your business as well.

How do you find the right people? The people you bring into your business to extend your offerings must mirror the values that beliefs that you hold for your business. If they interact with your clients, they must share your client philosophy. I have learned that the surest way to find good people is to ask for referrals from the right people—your inner circle of business associates whom you trust and respect.

Let's start with other consultants. You may want to form strategic alliances with other consultants to expand your offerings and your team. How do you find other consultants? Ask people whom you trust. You may find consultants through professional organizations that you belong to or through other professional networks. Once you identify another consultant with whom you want to collaborate in some way in your business, you must interview them to see if there is a good fit with your business. You should be able to answer each of the following questions:

- Do they share your client philosophy?
- Would you hire them?

- Would you refer them to a friend or client?
- Do they fit with your style and professional image?

If the answer to any one of those questions is no, then you should *not* bring them into your business. With other consultants, it is not enough to be able to answer these questions, you must also be sure that you have seen their work samples and how they perform the services that they offer. I suggest two cautions about bringing other consultants into your practice:

- Only align with consultants who provide complementary services—not direct competitors.
- Be willing to sever alliances with consultants who become problematic with your clients

Once you bring other consultants into your business you must protect your company by executing proper legal documents such as non-compete and confidentiality agreements.

The professionals whom you bring in your business may include certified public accountants and lawyers, webmasters, publicists, and virtual assistants. Finding the right people means that you have personnel who allow you to run your business and maximize your billable hours. The minute you discover that you are involved with professionals who interfere with this, it is time to sever the relationships. I have found the best way to find the right people is through networking, trade associations, government business certifying organizations, and referrals from other small businesses.

Hiring employees requires a much greater level of scrutiny. One challenge for very small consulting businesses is the time that it takes to manage the employee recruitment and selection process. You will want to advertise as well as ask for referrals. I have had great success hiring employees who began as interns from universities. The graduate programs provide screening of the students before placement. Hiring an intern provides a better sense of how well they align with your business and shape their development. I've also had success advertising for full-time positions in trade publications. The best employee I ever hired came through that source. Of course, keep in mind that you must follow all federal and state laws with regard to hiring protocols, especially as your business grows in size.

My worst mistake

I made what I believe is the biggest mistake I've ever made in my business when I hired the wife of one of my best clients. I was looking to hire a part-time administrative assistant who could also function as a marketing specialist. My client's wife was the ideal candidate—on paper—but I failed to trust my instincts. I called several references and could not get a positive reference on the candidate. I hired her anyway. She started off as a model employee but soon became a negative influence in our office. She knew that she had leverage because of her unique position and she took advantage by taking excessive time off. She became involved in unethical practices. I felt hamstrung because I knew instinctively that I should fire her but did not want to further jeopardize my client relationship. Before I could fire her she secretly took a contract with another existing client—literally stealing work—and left without notice. In one action, I lost an administrative assistant, lost one major client, and jeopardized another client relationship!

It goes without saying that sometimes the biggest mistakes can offer the greatest lessons. Here are the lessons that I learned that I will pass on to you:

- Always trust your intuition with regard to hiring employees or contracting with associates. If it does not feel right, then don't hire or contract with them.
- Never hire someone who is tied to a client.
- If you hire friends or family, use the same degree of scrutiny that you would apply to a stranger.
- Ask the right questions in the interview process to determine if the candidate shares your company values and client philosophy.
- Thoroughly check references.

6

SUSTAINABILITY

I never imagined, when I started in 1983, that I would be able to make a living out of the business that I created. What has compelled me to write this book is my gratitude to have a business that has met the needs of my family and me more than adequately through the worst recession of our modern time. This business that I have built, a consulting business, an intentional consulting practice, has been a good, sustainable business.

Why has my business been successful? We have evolved from a focus on public relations, to consulting and training, and now performance. Our evolution as a business is responsive to marketplace demands and our brand is consistent. The elements of sustainability for our business have been:

- demonstrated ethical business values
- consistent performance of quality work
- valuing our clients
- managing and protecting our brand
- responsible community service
- developing multiple streams of income and managing cash flows and debt
- managing through economic down cycles and recovery
- managing personal and business transitions

To stay in business you need to always have relevant services and products that people need. You need to be able to have products and services that leverage your offerings to extend yourself beyond your billable hours. You need to have a great team of people who are exceptional at representing your company and communicating your brand. You need to work harder for your client than you do for yourself. And you need to really care about your client. You need to manage your business operations, eliminate debt, and have great cash flow. Sustainable consultants seek ways to develop multiple streams of income and always monitor and reduce fixed costs. Intentional, sustainable consultants are active strategic planners and eliminate products and services that don't sell in the marketplace.

For the length of time that we've been in business we have weathered many economic down cycles and have learned strategies for managing through them. Each time we have emerged as a better, stronger business. Every time you have to go lean you find out what you're really made of and what you're really good at.

When I left the DuPont company, I started my company's primary services during an economic recession. Those services were in demand, and they are in demand now. But business has changed drastically during the time that we have been in business. It has required that we not only manage transitions of technology, but respond to the changes in the industry subsectors that we service and are a part of as well as the competitive issues that our own industry faces.

Business consultants must take the time to be reflective and reassess, remake, or even reposition their business when necessary. That is the key to managing transitions well and sustaining your business practice. The truth is that when it comes to economic down cycles that occur fairly regularly, probably about every 7–10 years, having a business that is countercyclical is a core strategy for survival. What services or products can you offer clients during a bad economy that they will need to buy?

During economic downturn, businesses avoid hiring employees and consumer spending drops, because consumers lack confidence. When businesses are not hiring new employees—and may be downsizing instead—training and development programs are less popular. However, greater emphasis is placed on efficiency and effectiveness, and organizational development consultants are needed to address these issues.

Our company has weathered at least three economic downturns and every time we have seen organizational decision-making impacted and connected to our survival. The key to survival has been the ability to still make contacts with decision-makers and businesses that are able to hire consultants to solve problems. Penetration of those companies becomes more difficult as employees and management are in a state of flux. However, this is why relationships are so important—those decision-makers with whom we have formed relationships over the years may find themselves in other companies. Our job is to be patient and supportive of our prospective clients. It also means that, during recession, we may have to engage in extended contract deliberation and negotiation.

Despite some of these changes in the contract/proposal negotiation process, price does not have to suffer. Clients are still willing to pay for the quality of work, the consultant's ability to solve the problem. The consultant/client relationship is still built on trust. Trust and the ability to perform will dictate the cost. Keep in mind that despite recession or economic downturn, new businesses form every day that are created as a result of a poor economic climate.

Economic Downturn is an Opportunity

If you are beginning consultant in the last 2 to 3 years you may have started your business because you saw an opportunity in the marketplace, or you may have started your business because you lost a job. Regardless of the reason you started your consulting, you may have an opportunity to pinpoint the work that you offer to meet the unique demand of recession minded clients. If you are an established business, use the economic downturn to find out what core business services and products drive your revenues.

What is your core business? How do you know? Now's the time to reassess your business. If you have been in business a few years, take a look at your products, services, and sales during the down cycles. For example, if your business is usually slow during the summer (or the winter) months, what are you still selling? If you had one year out of five that was a down year, what was it that you sold? Answering these questions will give you a clue to what core business services you have. In our case, I took a look back at our largest area of revenue in terms of services that we provide. And out of 20 services that we offer, five of our services brought in 85% of the revenue. This is the kind of analysis that you will need to do. What we learn from this exercise is our core services that make our company a sustainable business. In fact, I decided to discontinue a few of the services for which there was no demand, because I did not want them to drain our capacity.

I've stressed often throughout this book importance of having a strategic plan. In order to be sustainable you must not only evaluate your business plan but also maintain an updated strategic plan. If you been in business for while, take a look at your business plan.

- Is your market plan still relevant?
- Is your business rationale still relevant?
- Is your service area still relevant? When was the last time you completed a competitor analysis?
- Do you know who your competitors are? Most businesses are virtual today so your competition may have changed as well as your market. Do you know how you stand in these areas?

Seriously take the time to look at trends in the marketplace that may be affecting your core areas of service.

- Do you need more training?
- Another certification?
- Are you reaching the right clients?
- Do you need to change or tools or add new tools to your tool bag?
- Are there new industries or business areas that you could target?

Going through this exercise will provide you with information that will allow you to forecast potential growth areas and target prospective clients.

Conduct a financial analysis and review fixed costs. Take a look at some your largest clients and review your individual profit margins for specific jobs.

- Are you able to raise your fees?

- Does your service warrant increasing your fees?
- After you have reviewed your financial data are you able to determine what your most profitable product or service is?
- Can you offer more of this service or sell more products?
- What are the obstacles that prevent you from doing so?
- Are there other services or products that you should discontinue based on this review?

SWOT

Every consultant, whether you are new or have been in business for a while, should conduct a SWOT (strengths, weaknesses, opportunities and threats) analysis as part of your environmental scanning process of the strategic plan. First take a look at your strengths and weaknesses. This is your internal analysis. What are your strengths? What are your weaknesses? Then conduct an external analysis looking at opportunities based on current or future trends, and threats that might be able to put you out of business.

If you've done this analysis correctly you will be able to find your core strengths by extracting from your SWOT analysis and identifying your most profitable product or service in down times. Last, ask yourself the question what are you doing that you should not be doing, and what should you start? Then summarize this in 5–7 words. These services and products will be sustainable core offerings for your business. Seriously take the time to answer these questions for your company; you might want to include associates and clients in this process.

Understand your Value Proposition

Sustainable consultants are able to determine their value proposition by gathering information on their clients and solving their problems and meeting their needs. Business consultants must provide consistently excellent service and products in order to be perceived as adding value. That means spending time with your clients and learning their culture and becoming indispensable to them. Consultants who have high value become trusted partners of their clients. You know that you are providing value to your clients when your clients will not take action until they have spoken to you, when your clients seeks you out for your wisdom and guidance. Granted, you may not always be paid for the advice you offer, but you are available when needed. Base your fees on your perceived value.

"Your perceived value is never higher than when you have arrived at a long term relationship in which the client sees your wisdom as irreplaceable. In tough times clients cut expenses, not wisdom..."

Alan Weiss[11]

Managing Transitions

I have weathered many personal and business transitions that could have ended my business, but good planning and effective marketing prevented disaster for our business. I'd like to share a few examples of some transitions we made that could have jeopardized the business.

Too much income, too quickly

Our business grew tremendously in a two-year period, from 1996- 1998, which threw us into a high tax bracket; as a result, we owed a large amount of taxes. By 1998 my company has grown to have 4 employees and several contracted associates. I incorporated the business in 1995 and named officers for our corporation. I appointed an executive vice president and assumed the title of president and CEO and majority ownership. I sought the advice of a SCORE counselor who assisted me with business planning. With the counselor's advice, I decided to purchase commercial office space, as opposed to leasing it, to increase our expenses and provide a more cost-effective method to manage our taxes and increase my personal investment. Our company was able to obtain a commercial mortgage and purchase a historical center city duplex property, which had a tenant with a three-year lease in one of the buildings. The transition worked because it had little financial impact the first three years. We created a moving plan to minimize disruption to our business operation before making the transition from our leased space. We sent out press releases to publicize our move. This transition was smooth and well executed. The moving plan was a model for us and was activated in subsequent moves.

---

[11] Weiss, Alan (2009). *Million Dollar Consulting*, McGraw-Hill.

Opening a new office in a new location

A few years ago, I opened a second office outside of Denver, Colorado, in an attempt to grow our business in an expanded marketplace. Major business planning helped us to identify location and handle multiple moves that took place to open the second office. The primary strategies for the success of opening the new office was: networking with key business associations; obtaining business memberships in our new location; obtaining third-party certifications; marketing and promotions; and community involvement. All of these strategies eventually resulted in obtaining contracts. The biggest challenge was controlling communications relating to our headquarters so that our core marketplace did not feel abandoned or feel that our services had changed.

A client recently remarked that it did not matter to him where our office was because we always provided him with excellent client service.

Changing the structure

The 9/11 national crisis had a major impact on our business along with many others. It changed the way we did business because our government contracts were suddenly rescinded. Routine shipping of our products was halted, which had a direct impact on our income for a short period. The long-term impact was uncertain and required further changes in staffing so I laid off my full-time and part-time employees. I changed our business model to use contracted associates to support the consulting and training efforts. This has been a preferred model that has worked well.

Adding new products

New product development is a way to increase income and position the company as innovative. We established a business advisory council composed of our SCORE counselor and a client representing each service line of our business. This group provided feedback on every step of the way of our business expansion and our product launch. The key to the success of our new product line was to develop a specific plan, hire staff to manage it, and integrate it successfully in our business.

Personal transitions

You don't survive in business for long without dealing with personal crises. I've had my share of them. But the major learning I can share is that personal issues should not get in the way of the business. It is crucial to stay focused on the business on hand. There are some personal issues, such as illness, that can create serious challenges for a small business. This problem falls into the category of crisis planning. Every business ought to have systems in place where someone else whom you trust can take your place and make decisions until you recover.

Business Survival Tips

Here are a few business survival tips that I have accumulated over the years to use when times are lean. When the economy rebounds, these survival tips, if faithfully executed, will strengthen your business. I will address questions that have been presented to me.

What's the best way to be structured to stay up in economic slumps?

Independent consultants, whether they operate individually or as a practice should, follow the strategy of larger businesses and corporations during economic downturns. That means staying as lean as possible by reducing fixed costs, downsizing, and reducing inventory. If you have employees, you may want to consider laying them off or reducing staff through attrition. Hire other independent consultants for professional services as 1099 subcontractors. Not only will this reduce your employee expense, it will also reduce your other overhead costs associated with payroll management, benefits, marketing, mileage reimbursement, etc.

Another area where you can reduce expense is to work out of your house. This will reduce all costs associated with commutes and maintenance agreements. With regard to inventory, if you're a consultant who also sells products, consider strategies to reduce your inventory. Arrange with a third-party supplier to direct-ship products to your clients on an order-by-order basis. If you sell booklets or materials that need to be printed and assembled, consider finding a service provider online that can distribute materials directly to your clients. This will save personnel and shipping and handling costs.

Take a look at your utility costs and see if it is possible to bundle your services. You might decide that some of your bookkeeping services can be done by you or a part-time employee or associate who is already handling other work for you, such as administrative support. Look for ways to reduce all of your costs. You might also look at your meeting schedule with clients—can you schedule your appointments so that you use your time and gas more efficiently? Can you buy your supplies in bulk? Can you reduce your costs by recycling? Are you able to barter some of the services that you currently receive in exchange for others with another consultant? I have successfully partnered public relations services with another consulting firm. The other firm provide provided our company with publicist services, and we in turn conducted some of their client research.

How do you stay up after losing several clients? How do you sustain your energy?

Economic downturns can affect long-term client relationships. Over the last several years, we have seen several of our larger clients experience the major downsizing and mergers that are clearly part of an overall trend. In short, there are no surprises. We have learned that, in effective planning, we must always look at our largest accounts and have a plan in place should something happen to the steady and predictable income. The loss of a major account may even require you to seek temporary part-time employment for an extended period of time to replace the income until you're able to replace the client. We have experienced this several times with losses of our commissioned sales income and major clients. The development and launch of our own Spice of Life® product line was our attempt to minimize the anticipated loss of our largest client account and commissions from our product sales.

The way you sustain your energy is to remain optimistic, scan the environment for opportunities, and monitor the marketplace for other clients who may come along and replace that income. But you must be aggressive and you must plan ahead. You can never take a client or an account for granted.

How does your business plan or model respond to down cycles?

Although I have addressed business planning and strategic planning previously, it is essential that you constantly evaluate and re-visit your business plan. Is your business plan flexible? What aspects of your business are most vulnerable during the down cycle? What aspects of your business continue to flourish during economic down cycles? This is your strategy.

Take the time to consistently reach out to your core client base, and let them know what services you have to offer and your willingness to assist them. Never take a client for granted.

Why increase marketing and spend money you don't have?

During economic downturn, strategic marketing is your best investment of dollars. It will leverage what you do. Use this time to market and promote your brand or develop a brand strategy if you don't have one. Network to increase your visibility. Volunteer for causes that are consistent with your values and your company culture and tastefully publicize your efforts.

7

WHAT'S NEXT

Now that you have read all of the chapters in this book, it is time to focus on what's next. The best way to become an intentional consultant and grow a sustainable business is to begin today. Go back through the chapters of this book. Take your notepad and work through all of the exercises that have been shared here with you. Whether you are just starting out as a new consultant, or you have been in business for some time and you want to build your practice into a sustainable enterprise, make a commitment today to start doing the hard thing that most freelance consultants and very small businesses never do. PLAN.

My suggestion is that you set time aside every day to begin this process. Record your responses to these exercises in the same place so that you can read and reread them. It also may be useful for you to go through this process in as short a time as possible. Why not make it a 30-day commitment to become an intentional consultant and build a sustainable business? After you have completed all of the exercises, write and put in place an updated business and marketing plan. Develop a strategic plan for your business that incorporates all of the elements that have been discussed and presented here.

It is my hope that by sharing my personal story it will cut the time that it will take you develop and grow your sustainable practice. After all, what I have learned and shared here for your review has come through all of my trials and errors. That's not necessarily a bad thing, because most people know that without errors and missteps you will not experience success.

When you read my personal story from my early childhood through my academic and career development, my desire for entrepreneurship, and the germination and sustained growth of my consulting practice, there are some common themes that emerge.

I attribute my success to finding ways to narrow down all the noise, confusion, and negative influences, and to persist toward my vision of what I want for my life and business. This has meant staying focused on my own dream, not the dreams of others, and being willing to commit to a disciplined process of preparation, planning, reflection, and critique. Another aspect of my success strategy has been to seek outside verification of whether I am on the right path and provide the additional help, expertise, and support that I need to overcome obstacles and achieve my goals.

Last, I have a unique ability to not allow personal difficulties and challenges to derail me from my pursuits. In fact, when personal challenges have arisen my reaction is to remain strong, and use my inner will and spiritual drive, to give me even greater energy to pursue my goal.

Where Do I Go from Here?

Sometimes my clients will ask me, "What do you plan to do next? You have been in business for while—aren't you tired of consulting work and helping other organizations?" My answer is no, I'm not tired, I enjoy the work that I do, I love what I'm doing, and I'm living my dream. But what I do know that it is time to write a new chapter in my book and my own story. And as with any good business, a born entrepreneur knows it's worthwhile to look at new business ventures and new ideas.

I will begin by looking backwards, in order to look forward; this is the best way to begin any reflective process and search for new ideas. Seasoned business consultants should take the time to mine the knowledge from their business to develop the underpinnings of what may be their legacy. If you've been in business for a long time, as I have, then it's time to look over the body of work that you have completed and determine what might be useful for others who might follow in your path.

My philosophy is one where I always feel obligated to give and share with others. This book, *The Intentional Consultant*, is part of that philosophy. When you go through the process of knowledge-mining your business, you will be able to see what you have created and contributed to others and to society at large, and perhaps what might be next for you.

It may be that your reflection causes you to look at opportunities to build succession for family members to someday inherit your practice. Or you may discover that you may want to sell it, but you can only sell your consulting practice if it is really a sustainable business with regular accounts and goodwill that have some sort of market value. Could aspects of your business be developed into a franchise?

The skills that you've learned as an intentional consultant, which have built a sustainable business practice, can be applied to any business venture. If you are successful in your consulting practice and you are in the top 4% who were able to make a six-figure salary with limited overhead costs, then you may be in a position to save some of your excess revenues for future business investment. Business investments beyond the actions you take to solidify your own wealth, such as retirement planning, might allow you to expand your practice; you could begin another business to multiply your streams of income.

- What might those other business ventures be?
- Do you want to get into retail?
- Would you want to be a writer?
- Are you interested in a and Internet-based business?
- Or are you ready to go back and earn an additional academic degree or credential?

Only you know the answers to these questions, but setting time aside for true reflection is the only way that will get you there.

Generating New Ideas

You will need to go through your own creative process to begin to generate new ideas. The best way to come up with new ideas is not to pressure yourself to do so but to give yourself a chance to think about possibilities. Take a look at a service or product you already offer. Can it be sold to a different kind of client? Changed in some way to create a new product or service? When you go through your strategic planning process, you will be identifying new trends in the marketplace. Part of your SWOT analysis will have you identify present and future business opportunities. Start with that.

Place yourself in new areas of business, new people, new places. Read. Get inspired. Talk to children. Create a new "idea" folder and begin to capture your ideas. Carry "post-it" notes in your purse or briefcase and jot those ideas down when they come to you and collect those ideas. Keep your iPad and smart phone handy to add to your idea lists.

After a month or so, take a look in your folder of ideas and put all of your ideas together. See if you can boil those ideas down to 5–7 really great ones. These ideas might be the seeds of a new business. Now it's time to begin to ask others what their ideas are, as discussed in Chapter 2. If you think your ideas are proprietary, be careful not to share them with people you don't trust or have them complete a non-disclosure form. Remember, for any new enterprise you begin, follow the steps that I have shared with you in this book.

You will always have obstacles that will get in the way of achieving your dream. The obstacles may prevent you from germinating the seed of a dream that you believe can grow into a sustainable practice. Don't give up or become discouraged. Remain vigilant and persistent so that you can fully reap the harvest you have sown. Great success to you now and into the future.

It's time for me to walk my talk and begin my own process of reflection and exploration.

ABOUT THE AUTHOR

Dr. Devona Williams founded Goeins-Williams Associates, Inc., (GWA) a successful performance consulting business, in 1986 to "help organizations achieve greater productivity in strategic work environments." As President/CEO of GWA, Dr. Williams has contributed her talents to helping more than 40,000 individuals in hundreds of organizations increase their performance and effectiveness. GWA focuses on *People, Process and Performance*™ and works with clients to develop solutions to meet organizational and individual objectives and achieve lasting results. The company provides a range of consulting services including assessments, focus groups, strategic planning, meeting facilitation, organizational and individual development.

Williams is a frequent keynote speaker on business, diversity, leadership, motivation, and success and contributing author to the inspirational book, *Remarkable Women*, and creator of the national best selling Spice of Life® Diversity Card training tool. GWA was named a Top 100 MBE in the region including Virginia, Maryland, and Delaware. The *Denver Business Journal* and the *Delaware Today* magazine recognized GWA as an Outstanding Woman-Owned business and won a Superstars in Business award by the Delaware State Chamber of Commerce. Williams holds a doctorate in Urban Affairs & Public Policy from the University of Delaware and is an experienced assistant professor of Community Development and Leadership at the University of Delaware's School of Urban Affairs. Williams is a recipient of the University of Delaware's Presidential Citation for Outstanding Achievement and Distinguished Alumna Award from the University's College of Urban Affairs & Public Policy.